William M. Gaines's

RAVING

MAD®

Albert B. Feldstein, Editor

**WARNER
PAPERBACK
LIBRARY**

A Warner Communications Company

WARNER PAPERBACK LIBRARY EDITION
First Printing: September, 1973

Title "MAD" used with permission of its owner,
E.C. Publications, Inc.

This Warner Paperback Library Edition is published
by arrangement with E.C. Publications, Inc.

Warner Paperback Library is a division of Warner Books, Inc.,
75 Rockefeller Plaza, New York, N.Y. 10019.

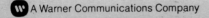 A Warner Communications Company

CONTENTS

Children's books are enjoying unprecedented popularity these days. Mainly because they're being bought by parents! However, we've got a sneaking suspicion that the kids aren't too thrilled with them. Let's face it: "A Hole is to dig," "A Pony is to ride on," and "A Mommy is to love you" is just so much saccharine and slush. Today's kid will someday be reading Hemingway and Faulkner—not books by ladies with three names. He wants truth . . . and realism—not goody-goody namby-pambyisms. He wants books that describe the "real" world around him. Something like the following sample . . . MAD's own version of . . .

A REALISTIC CHILDRE N'S

...for realistic

A HOLE IS
WHAT YOU NEED
THIS BOOK LIKE
IN YOUR HEAD

MODERN DEFINITIONS FOR THE MODERN CHILD

BY PEARL AND GARY BELKIN
ILLUSTRATED BY JOE ORLANDO

BOOK

children

A Mother is to hide behind when Daddy gets mad at you..

A Grandmother is to spoil you.

A Tantrum is to throw in front of a Grandmother so she'll holler at your mother and then spoil you more.

A Father is to give you long lectures about
how wonderful he was when he was a boy.

A Toy Store is to stop in front of when
Grandpa takes you for a walk.

Tears are to get your own way.

A Brother is to blame things on.

An Uncle is when he pinches your cheek, you're not allowed to pinch back.

An Aunt is to give you clothes for your birthday, instead of toys.

A Sister is to blame things on you.

A Teacher is to lose patience with you.

Open School Week is when your crabby teacher smiles a lot.

A Cold is to stay home from school with.

Medicine is to yecch after taking.

Table Manners are for when there are guests for dinner.

Dinner is to push around on the plate until it's such a mess that even your mother doesn't want you to eat it.

A Pet is to scream and holler until they get you one; but they never get you a monkey.

Goldfish are to overfeed.

A Bird is to bury.

Water is to ask for just when they think you've fallen asleep.

A Cookie is what you don't get because it will spoil your dinner, or because you didn't finish your dinner.

Mother's Day is for Daddy to buy Mommy a present and say it's from you.

A Baby Sitter is a girl who gets 75¢ an hour to watch your TV set.

Camp is to write home for money from.

A Museum is where parents take you instead of someplace good.

Homework is to do if there's nothing on television.

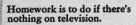

Gloves are to
lose one of.

A Piano is to practice loud on when your mother is trying to make a phone call so she'll tell you to go out and play.

An Allowance is to get an advance on.

A Movie Theater is to make noise in and put your feet on the seats until the matron comes.

Love Scenes are to giggle at.

Other kid's toys are to share.

Mud is to track
into the house.

A Girl is to
pull her hair.

A Kiss is to
wipe off.

Don Martin, MAD's maddest artist—and known to his analyst as the original "Freudian Slip"—tells us about one of his recent sessions

In The Psychiatrist's Office

END

Classified ad writers for the daily newspapers seem to go off into a world all their own when it comes to using abbreviations in their copy. In most cases, they carry this business of abbreviating so far that the reader has his hands full trying to figure out what in heck the ad means. To assist in his arduous task, the Editors now present . . .

A MAD GUIDE TO CLASSIFIED ADVERTISING ABBREVIATIONS

H-T Sdn.—
Here's trouble for some dunce

2-tn.rd&crm.—
2 tons of rusted and corroded metal

r.&h.—
rattles and heaves

w/w—
wheels wobble

auto.trans.—
auto transportable, but not under
    its own power

pw.st.—
probably was stolen

bod. per.—
body perforated with bullet holes

lw.mlg.—
law men looking for it

pt. Fr. Poodle—
pretty Fierce Poodle

6 mo.—
6 razor-sharp molars

b.&w.—
belligerent & wild

ml.—
bites mailmen

vic.—
vicious

lib.rew.—
liberal reweaving of trouser seat
necessary if he gets behind you

Help Wanted—Male

CPA, hd.bkp., exp. Fd. Inc. Tx.,
M.S.pref., yg.&amb., fl/pt time,
st.nec.Sal., Wimbogger Corp.
259 Main St. PQ-2-3456

CPA—
Corrupt Price Adjustor

hd.bkp.—
to head off bankruptcy

exp.Fd.Inc.Tx.—
expert at Faking due Income Taxes

M.S.pref.—
Man from Sing-Sing preferred

yg.&amb.—
Yugoslavian and ambidextrous

fl/pt time—
looking for a fool to putter away
time

st.nec.Sal.—
start by necking with Sally, who will
be your secretary

25

ATTR. CON. BUNG.—
Atrocious Construction Bungle

2 b.r.—
2 broken rainspouts

l.r.—
leaky roof

frm. dn. r.—
farmyard drains into rear

2 car. gar. att.—
2 carloads of garbage in attic

fl. bsmt.—
flooded basement

f. p. $19,000—
fantastic profit at $19,000

lo. dn.—
low down neighborhood

FHA Mort.—
Faces Harold's Mortuary

END

With our population exploding, and the building business booming, and our cities expanding into suburbs, and our suburbs expanding into other suburbs, it won't be long before the entire U.S.A. will be one solid hunk of concrete from border to border and ocean to ocean. And then, that good old American family sport, "The Picnic," will be as dead as last week's Rock 'n Roll hit. So, for the benefit of our great-grandchildren, who may be interested in what things were like in the good old days, here is

A MAD LOOK AT PICNICS

28

30

31

32

I hate paper plates! The wind is always blowing them away!

Not these! Somebody came out with a simple and clever gadget. They've got a piece of **adhesive tape** on the bottom!

. . . so no matter how **strong** the wind gets, the paper plates **stick** to the **table cloth**!

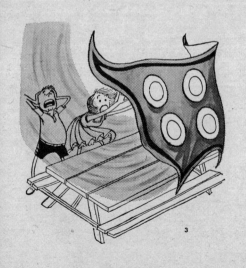

END

45

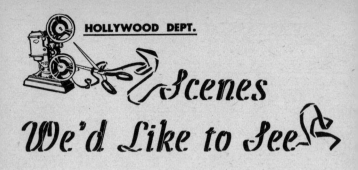

Scenes We'd Like to See

The Launching

49

With this article, MAD introduces a new feature, based on the proposition that you can tell an awful lot about a person by the scraps of paper and cards and bills and photographs and money he carries around in his wallet. Since we are all basically nosey, we thought it would be exciting to see what *famous people* carried around in *their* wallets. So we sent out a special research team to pick some famous pockets. They recently returned with three laundry tickets and four black eyes. We'll be sending them out again for the next issue (when they recover), but in the meantime, we'd like to present *our* version of what you'd *probably find* in this "first of a series" revealing the unexpected contents of . . .

CELEBRITIES' WALLETS!

"Mack the Knife"
instructions on how to sing it:
Oh, THE SHARK BITES—
(snap fingers twice)
WITH HIS TEETH DEAR—
(snap fingers twice)
AND IT LEAVES THEM—
(take two steps toward audience)
PEARLY WHITE!
(shout, snap fingers, and smear)
SCARLET BILLOWS—
(take two steps back)

SCHLOCK PUBLISHERS
48 West 60th Street
New York City 93, N. Y.
I enclose $3.95. Please send
me copy of your new book:
"*HOW TO BE POPULAR*"
NAME BOBBY DARIN
ADDRESS HOLLYWOOD
CITY — STATE CALIF.
PLEASE RUSH!

Grauman's Chinese Theater
HOLLYWOOD, CALIFORNIA

Mr. Bobby Darin   July 18. 1961
Hollywood, Calif.

Dear Mr. Darin:
   This is to advise you that we have con-
tacted our lawyers, and they are prepared
to bring suit against you for the scene
you created in front of our world famous
theater last Wednesday evening.
   Imagine! Pouring fresh cement, and trying to leave your footprints next to
those of great movie stars of the past!
And without our permission!

                          Sincerely,

                    東團美貝酋

          For Grauman's Theat

Schwab's Drug Store
2908 Sunset Blvd. Hollywood, Cal.

"The Drug Store Of The Stars"

Charge to:
Mr. Bobby Darin

4 Pair "Actor-Type" Sunglasses $12.00

LLOYDS of LONDON

79 Lutine Street, London W.1

July 28, 1961

Mr. Bobby Darin
Hollywood, Calif.

Dear Mr. Darin:

    We have received your letter
containing your request for "Special
Insurance". Although Lloyd's has a
reputation for insuring just about
everything, we cannot write a policy
to insure your "Greatness." As you
can understand, this is a rather un-
usual request, even for an enter-
tainer from America. Perhaps we can
do business when you have something
a bit more tangible you would like
to insure.

             Faithfully yours,

Horace Wickwire

Horace Wickwire
Special Policy Div.

STANLEY B. GITTELSON, M.D.
Suite 2345 Medical Arts Bldg.
Beverly Hills, California

July 12, 1961

Dear Mr. Darin:-

The results of your X-ray and physical examination show nothing conclusive, except that you have a minor abrasion of the thumb. This may be due to excessive finger-snapping. Try to cut down on this activity in the next few weeks, if you can. As for your other complaint, I cannot find any medical or physical cause for the recent sudden increase in your hat-size. I suggest that it may be a psychological phenomenon, considering all the facts, including what I've read about you. I would be glad to recommend a qualified

STEVE BLAUNER

Bobby Baby:-
Enclosed are some more photos of him (Sinatra) singing. You've almost got him down to a "T"—. Keep practicing, and soon they won't be able to tell the difference—
                    Steve Baby—

PERSONAL MANAGEMENT

END

54

USING THE SAME PRINCIPAL DEPT.

Our educational systems have a sneaky little gimmick (as far as the kids are concerned) called "Open School Week"—or "Open School Night"—in which the parents of the students are invited to come in and discuss their sons' and daughters' progress and problems with their teachers. As champions of justice, we believe that turnabout is fair play, and business organizations should invite children of parents to come in and discuss their Daddies' and Mommies' progress and problems with their bosses. In short, they ought to have

OPEN OFFICE WEEK

ORGANIZATION ENTERPRISES CORPORATION, INC.
12345 Conformity Way   Businessville, U.S.A.
TOgetherness 2-2222

October 26th 1961

Dear Children:

Every year at this time, ORGANIZATION ENTERPRISES CORPORATION, INC., invites the offspring of our employees to visit our offices. This year, we have designated the week of October 30th 1961 as "Open Office Week."

Your Daddy's Department Head is looking forward to meeting you personally, and discussing your Daddy with you. Should you have any further questions concerning how he is getting along, I will also be available to talk things over with you during that week.

Hoping to see you soon, I remain,
Yours truly,

E. J. Organization

E. J. Organization
Chairman of the Board

P.S. Naturally, this invitation is also extended to those children whose mommies work for us, too.--EJO

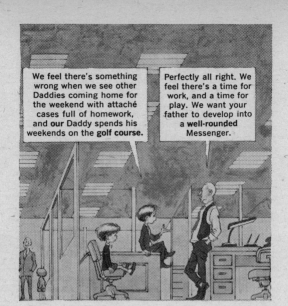

One thing bothers me. Last week, I asked him what the company makes, and my Daddy didn't **know**. Shouldn't he care enough to even **ask**?

He might be afraid. This company is so large and diversified, nobody really knows what we make or do. You see, Daddies of your father's age have a basic need for security. He might be **afraid** to ask because they might find out we're not doing anything and **fire** all of us.

64

65

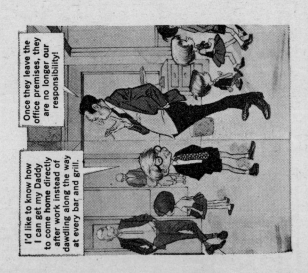

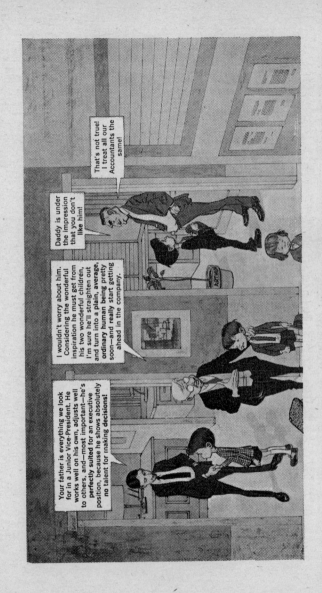

69

VENGEANCE

BY ANTONIO PROHIAS

END

Television has only been in general use for about 15 years, and yet it has completely changed our way of life. The TV set has brought the world into our living rooms—as if we didn't have enough troubles already. It has wised-up our young people beyond their years, killed the ancient art of conversation, and reduced the pastime of reading to the pages of "TV Guide." We at MAD have always found television a vulnerable target for our kidding. But somehow, we've limited our fun to the idiotic things that appear <u>on</u> the TV screen, and we've ignored the idiotic things that <u>face</u> the TV screen. mainly, the TV viewers, some of whom can be more ridiculous than all the ridiculous TV programs and TV commercials combined. To them MAD dedicates the following article, which offers . . .

the
lighter side of

THE
TELEVISION
SET

Click

3

4

THE
EARLY
EARLY
SHOW

5

6

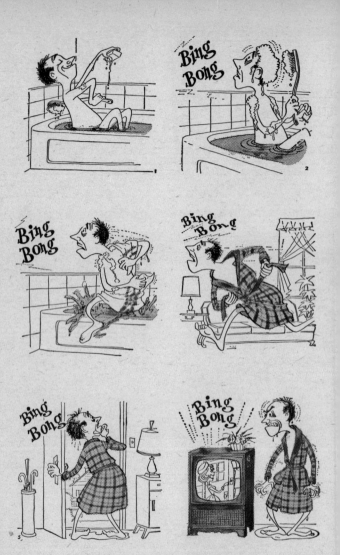

Ever notice how Doctors try to impress patients by leaving medical journals around their waiting rooms? MAD feels they should forget their "hypocritic" oath, and leave *honest* publications around, like

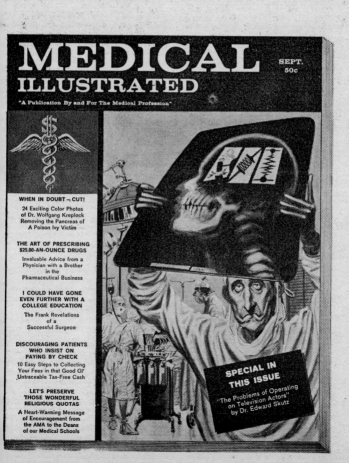

MEDICAL ILLUSTRATED

SEPT. 50c

"A Publication By and For The Medical Profession"

WHEN IN DOUBT — CUT!

24 Exciting Color Photos of Dr. Wolfgang Kreplock Removing the Pancreas of A Poison Ivy Victim

THE ART OF PRESCRIBING $25.00-AN-OUNCE DRUGS

Invaluable Advice from a Physician with a Brother in the Pharmaceutical Business

I COULD HAVE GONE EVEN FURTHER WITH A COLLEGE EDUCATION

The Frank Revelations of a Successful Surgeon

DISCOURAGING PATIENTS WHO INSIST ON PAYING BY CHECK

10 Easy Steps to Collecting Your Fees in that Good Ol' Untraceable Tax-Free Cash

LET'S PRESERVE THOSE WONDERFUL RELIGIOUS QUOTAS

A Heart-Warming Message of Encouragement from the AMA to the Deans of our Medical Schools

SPECIAL IN THIS ISSUE

"The Problems of Operating on Television Actors" by Dr. Edward Skutz

Dear Dr. Grepps

If any of you doctor-readers have questions about your profession you'd like answered, contact Dr. Grepps, care of this magazine. There will be a $5 charge for all questions brought to Dr. Grepps' office. However, if you'd like Dr. Grepps to visit your home to pick up your question, his fee is $10

Q. I don't know what's the matter with me lately. I've become awfully sloppy and forgetful. After sewing up my patients, I always seem to have some silly little thing left over. A liver, a gall bladder, a navel, things like that. This absent-mindedness on my part is very embarrassing to me. What should I do?

A. Lovelace, M.D.
Tacoma, Wash.

A. Use care and discretion. After each operation, have another physician or nurse double-check you. Then, if you *still* find yourself having things left over after operations, you owe it to yourself and to humanity to give up your career, and start writing authoritative medical articles for the *Reader's Digest.*

Q. I can't tell you how much I enjoyed "Seventy-Five Obnoxious Ways to Harass The Police With Your MD License Plates" by Dr. Norbett Noodnik in your August issue. His tips to other doctors on the art of parking in Restricted Zones, on sidewalks, and on Safety Islands while pretending to be on calls but actually attending poker sessions or going bowling were simply marvelous. What ever happened to Dr. Noodnik?

R. S. Bladder, M.D.
Lincoln, Neb.

A. Last week, Dr. Noodnik paid a house call to a patient across the street from his office, and he was arrested for jay-walking.

Q. I am planning to take a two-week vacation very shortly. Can you give me the names of some substitutes whom I can have cover for me and see my patients until I get back? Naturally, I wouldn't want these substitutes to be too good, since I'd hate to lose all my patients to them permanently and have no practice to come home to.

B. T. Salivate, M.D.
Madison, Wisc.

A. General Practitioners in your area usually rely upon the following three men to handle their practices when they are on vacation: Dr. Benjamin Oliver, % Oliver's Clinic for Parakeets; Mr. Hiram Blecher, % Blecher's Butcher Shop; and Mr. William "Shaky" Huntz, % Chapter 23 of Alcoholics Anonymous (if not there, try Barney's Bar and Grill).

Q. I am a young lady who reads your magazine occasionally. All my life, I've been told that doctors make the most desirable husbands. Well, I've gone out with several doctors, and I've found them

to be so tied up in their profession that they know absolutely nothing about the world outside it. In reality, they are shallow, dull bores, and many of them can't even utter a simple, intelligent, gramatically-correct sentence.

Miss Coral Frost
New York City

A. I possibly cannot imagine, of all places, where this false impression, you got it from, at.

Q. I have just opened an office as a General Practitioner. Would you kindly advise me as to the correct rules to follow for referring patients to Specialists, no matter how minor their ailments are? Also, what is a fair kickback to expect from the specialist when I do this?

A. C. Hacklehead, M.D.
Atlanta, Ga.

A. Send all patients with complaints from the neck up to "Eye, Ear, Nose and Throat" Specialists. Refer all patients with ailments from the waist to the neck to "Heart Specialists." Send all patients with problems from the waist to the toes to "Chiropodists." Refer all patients with ailments in any other areas to "Veterinarians." Regarding your second question, a fair kickback fee is 25% of the Specialist's regular fee, or whatever else you can wheedle out of him—whichever is higher.

Q. I am a nice, middle-aged lady who absolutely adores the ground my doctor walks upon. I mean, as far as I'm concerned, he can do no wrong. He is kind, and good, and intelligent. Sometimes, I don't believe he's real. To me, he's like a brilliant, happy sun shining down on a dark sick world. I'm planning to write a book about him. Can you suggest a title?

Mrs. P. K. Kimball,
Portland, Me.

A. How about "My Doctor, The Sun"?

Q. What is the all-time record for a General Practitioner turning simple phone inquiries into expensive visits to his office?

J. L. Jukes, M.D.
Roanoke, Va.

A. In one week during 1958, Dr. Harry Gideons, of Passaic, N.J., convinced 71 people who phoned him to come to his office. They included: 28 people with minor colds; 18 people with slight headaches; a representative from a TV survey asking him what program he was watching; his wife, whom he only charged half-fee; a kidnapper, asking ransom for the doctor's son; and 22 wrong numbers.

81

Every month, MEDICAL ILLUSTRATED presents another citizen who most closely typifies the average American patient. Our patient this month is Selwyn Abisch, of Tulsa, Oklahoma. Here is the day in Mr. Abisch's life which made him the typical American Patient for September.

Meet...
Selwyn Abisch
MEDICAL ILLUSTRATED'S
"Patient of the Month"

Mr. Abisch arrived at the office of Dr. Donald Fleespit at 10:00 AM for his annual check-up. While thumbing through such typical doctor's waiting room publications as **Liberty, Colliers'** and **Poor Richard's Almanac,** his shoes were stepped on by 12 screaming kids.

At 12:00 Noon, Mr Abisch was ushered into Small Examination No. 1 by the nurse, where he was told to remove all his clothes. Unknown to Abisch, Dr. Fleespit sneaked into Small Examination Room No. 2 to avoid him and another patient in Small Examination Room No. 3.

At 1:00 PM, Abisch was led into Small Examination Room No. 2 by the same nurse. In the nick of time, Dr. Fleespit avoided Abisch by sneaking back into Small Examination Room No. 1. The patient in Small Examination Room No. 3, meanwhile,was moved up a notch to Small Examination Room No. 4.

At 2:15 PM, Abisch was ushered into Small Examination Room No. 3. In this room, Abisch bumped into a female patient, also completely undressed, who immediately fled to Small Examination Room No. 5. Meanwhile, Dr. Fleespit avoided both of them, and twelve other patients, by sneaking into Small Examination Room No. 6.

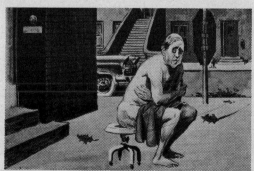

At 4:30, still undressed and yet to be examined, Abisch was ushered through another door. This one led to Large Examination Room No. 7 — also known as "The Street". Here, due to overexposure, Abisch caught double pneumonia.

At 8:00 PM, Dr. Fleespit paid a house call on Abisch, and picked up twice the fee he would have gotten had Abisch been able to trap him into an examination in his office. Which is what Dr. Fleespit was angling for all day.

84

Fill Your Doctor's Bag With Fancy Useless Gadgets
AND IMPRESS YOUR
PATIENTS!

Let's face it, Docs! Outside of a stethoscope and a few throat sticks, what else do you need for a house call? Not very much! But you can't visit a patient with a practically empty Doctor's Bag! How would it look? And how much could you charge? Now, you can fill your bag with a dazzling array of complicated gadgets to impress patients and make them receptive to those exorbitant fees—with a

SMEED

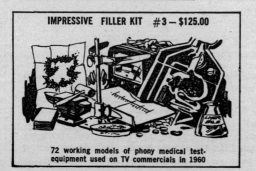

YOUR PRESCRIPTION HANDWRITING
—The Key To Your Personality

BY *[signature]* M.D.

Each month, MEDICAL ILLUSTRATED presents three samples of handwriting excerpts collected at random from prescriptions filled out by doctors around the country, with a personality analysis of each by the noted physician, handwriting-expert, and stock market player, Doctor Clarence Fink.

SAMPLE NO. 1

[handwriting sample]

As you can see, Dr. Martin Klutts, of Lincoln, Neb., has an extremely forceful and precise handwriting. Note the bold "u's," the sturdy "s," and the crisp "p" in the above words "cough syrup." They indicate a strong personality, one which would have the courage to charge as much as $50.00 for filling out a child's school check-up form. More chicken-hearted physicians with weaker "h's" and "y's" than those shown in example above, wouldn't dare to charge more than $35.00.

SAMPLE NO. 2

[handwriting sample]

Observe the way Dr. Kenneth Dibbler, of Dover, Del., clips and chops his words. Pay particular attention to the clear, but abruptly cut word "Aspirin." Dr. Dibbler undoubtedly loves to slice things, especially human tissue. His steady and well-rounded "p" however (above) tells me that he is a fine surgeon. I'd wager that at least two out of the three patients he operates on for athlete's foot survive.

SAMPLE NO. 3

cold tablets

We had intended to feature a sample of the prescription handwriting of Dr. David Pferd, of Dallas, Tex., but unfortunately we were unable to find anything he has written, except for the above unintelligent, illegible gibberish. It is naturally impossible to analyze this kind of scribbling, since it makes no sense. I strongly believe the above are some scratch lines the doctor made while testing a new ball-point pen.

TEST YOUR
BEDSIDE MANNER

As every physician knows, a good bedside manner is one of the most important qualities of modern medical practice. To improve yours, every issue we present a hypothetical case. Study it carefully, then decide how you would treat it with good bedside manner, and check your answer against the correct procedure indicated below

This patient has just fallen off the roof of an 8-story building. He was dragged into his bed screaming in pain, and suffering from 114 broken bones, several crushed ribs, internal injuries, and several forms of concussion. What is the first thing you should do upon entering his room?

Answer: Sit down on a chair next to his bed, take out a long sheet of paper, remove your pen from your pocket, unscrew the cap, and ask him if he has ever had measles, mumps, chicken pox, whooping cough, scarlet fever, acne, and ninety-eight other irrelevant childhood diseases.

HEARD THROUGH THE STETHOSCOPE

by Doc Windish

News and Gossip Along Medicine Avenue

Confidential to Dr. F. H.: You're new in the profession, so perhaps you can be excused for the horrible way you botched up your bill to Ferdinand Muffty. In the future, try to remember that when your patient has Blue Shield, you automatically add at least $100 to your regular exorbitant fee!

Doctor Ira Ossified, of Los Angeles, Cal. being broken from physician to intern by Dr. Paul Heaps, officer of the AMA. Dr. Ossified's waiting room was found to contain a copy of the National Geographic which was less than eight years old.

Send a "Cheer-up Note" to Dr. Gary Skegg, of Salt Lake City, Utah. He made less than $35,000 last year!

* * * *

This year's annual $5000 AMA award for the "Best Definition of Socialized Medicine" goes to Dr. Thomas Thuggins, of Concord, N. H. Dr. Thuggins' prize-winning definition: "Socialized Medicine is when you have to charge a patient less than $25 for a one-minute office visit." How true! How true!

* * * *

Why are Dr. George Floobush and his lovely nurse, Goldie, staying after office hours these days, hmmm? They claim it's to forge X-ray photos for Dr. Floobush's booming phony accident insurance business. But WE know differently, don't we? . . . There wasn't a dry eye at the Ritz-Neuman Hotel last Friday night when the very, very busy Dr. Fenwick Zemmst was introduced to his lovely wife, Hermione, during their 15th wedding anniversary celebration. Many, many more happy years of bliss, you two!

*. * * *

Because of the business recession, I've just learned that the AMA Lobby in Washington will be cut drastically. Starting this Fall, the Lobby will be operating in the nation's capital with a skeleton force of only 55,000 men!

* * * *

Four-year-old Ronnie Goulart's announcement in this column last month that he was planning on entering Medical School in 1980 brought only 106,927 marriage proposals from mothers of three-year-old girls. Perhaps the recent bad weather around the country delayed the rest of the mail! . . . How about dropping a line to another lonely physician fighting for Uncle Sam? I'm referring, of course, to Dr. Harry Pepper, of White Plains, N. Y. The 24-year-old Dr. Pepper typifies the American physician who must give up a comfortable and lucrative practice to struggle through the ranks of the rugged U.S. Army. Address all mail to: Brig. Gen. Harold Pepper, U.S. Medical Corps, Special Assignment, Waldorf-Astoria Hotel, New York City.

* * * *

Sorry to hear that Dr. Terrance Mittigan lost his General Practitioner's license last week for incompetence, medical ignorance, sloppy examinations, and inability to write a prescription. Good luck in your new career as a "Specialist," Terry!

Fun-loving Dr. Michael Compain is at it again! That crazy, waggish nut is convulsing doctors and nurses at Westside Maternity Hospital these days with his latest antics. Get this: Mike is running through the wards where momentarily-expecting mothers are confined, shouting, "All right! Somebody get me plenty of cold water and dirty sheets!" Don't ever lose that sense of humor, Mike ... it's worth a million dollars!

* * * *

In commemoration of "Work Hand-In-Hand With Your Local Pharmacist Month," the AMA is sponsoring a series of closed-circuit TV lectures. Purpose is to overcome the dreadful habit too many patients have of using up left-over $30-an-ounce drugs from one illness, for another illness a few weeks later — instead of buying a new batch. Next Tuesday's lecture will be entitled, "Prescribing Expensive Drugs Which Must Be Used Up In 24 Hours Or They Lose All Their Potency."

Mrs. Herman Hemprope, of Newark, New Jersey, and her marriage-hungry daughter, Bernice, returning from a very successful 2-week vacation at the Hotel Zilch-Plaza, in Ferndale, New York.

Dr. and Mrs. Thurston Biffle shopping for drapes at Saks Fifth Avenue. (This unimportant news item was inserted solely as a favor to Mrs. Biffle, the status-seeking physician's wife. She still can't get over how the thrilling words "Dr. and Mrs." sound!) . . . Dr. Paul Whistfield, of Nashville, Tenn., will never live down the embarrassing thing that happened to him in his office last week. While being paid a surprise visit by his friend, Dr. Kevin Portside, Dr. Whistfield was caught red-handed actually trying to READ one of the 800 medical books he keeps on display to impress his patients. It's the best laugh the medical profession has had in years!

* * * *

END

Don Martin spent some time in prison recently due to a typographical error. His papers read: "Admit Mr. Martin to the Big House" instead of "Admit Mr. Martin to the Bug House"! Before the mistake could be rectified, and Don could be sent on to the proper institution for observation, he did some observing of his own. For example, he watched:

The Prison Mess Hall Riot

END

Ever since the end of World War II, it has been considered quite stylish, for Americans to adopt some of the tradition of Oriental culture—such as Judo, Zen Bhuddism, Sukiaki, and Horn-Rimmed Glasses. The latest Japanese import is a rugged form of physical combat in which the participants employ ancient and respected Oriental techniques, like slapping, kicking, biting, eye-gouging and rabbit punching. In other words—fighting dirty! This sport is known as

"KARATE"

TEETH EXTRACTED 5 YEN

The prime ingredient of this sport is a highly-developed degree of "kime" or "focus," in which all the body's strength is momentarily channeled into one isolated area — such as the finger tip.

CHOOSE ONE FROM COLUMN "A" AND ONE FROM COLUMN "B"

A	B
BROKEN ARM	MASHED KIDNEY
CRACKED VERTEBRA	CRUSHED RIB
RUPTURED SPLEEN	INNA LABONZA

Despite its violent appearance, the true goal of Karate lies in achieving a state of absolute calm and serenity.

In the cloistered tranquility of Tokyo "Dojos," Karate disciples spend long hours in philosophical discussions.

Students claim this ancient art is an opportunity to contemplate nature at close range — like f'rinstance, stars!

TIMBER!

99

Actually, serious students of Karate will rarely engage in physical combat with one another, preferring to test their highly-developed skills on inanimate objects instead, such as boards, rocks, and nails. This is partially because they do not wish to inflict injury on another living being, but mainly because boards, rocks, and nails can't fight back!

BOARDS **ROCKS**

NAILS

"I KNOW I CAN DO IT . . . THEREFORE I CAN DO IT!" By implanting positive, convincing thoughts such as this one firmly in his mind, the Karate student is capable of performing incredible feats of strength and physical prowess.

Before attempting to split the anvil with his bare hand, Karate student prepares himself for the feat psychologically.

Sufficiently confident of capability, Karate student brings edge of his hand down sharply, splitting anvil in two.

Closer examination of shattered pieces reveals WHY Karate student knew that he could split anvil in two all along.

As with many other Oriental rites, the prelude to a Karate exhibition involves traditional rituals, and incantations, burning of incense, scattering of salt to the four winds, and taking side bets. Below, we see a part of the elaborate ceremony performed by a student prior to driving a nail through a 4-inch plank with his bare foot.

• Karate student first scatters rice on ground. This ritual signifies manhood.

Student then covers the rice with salt, signifying strength and determination.

Student then eats the rice with salt, signifying Karate don't pay very good.

Student next performs series of low bows to each point of compass. Not only does this ritual symbolize humility, but also helps him find any grains of rice he may have missed.

Close study of hands reveals ancient Oriental expression of student's inner confidence.

Closer study of hands reveals ancient Occidental expression —thrown in for good measure.

At the start of the actual feat, the student must remember to "kime" all of his strength into the point of his toe.

When the force of the blow drives the nail through the mahogany board, the student must remember to ignore pain.

HOW KARATE CAN BE USED AROUND THE HOUSE

NO MORE CAN OPENER

NO MORE SKILLET

NO MORE HAMMER

When nail turns out to be wrong one, student must remember to take pedicure before he tries next Karate exhibition.

NO MORE SAW

NO MORE CHISEL

NO MORE WORK

One of the reasons for the upsurge to interest in Karate is that many practical uses may be found for this ancient art by applying its various facets to everyday situations.

AT THE BEACH

You are embarrassed in front of your girl by a bully who keeps kicking sand in your face, and calling you "skinny."

With Karate, through the means of "kime," you just direct all of your strength and energy down into your left foot.

That way, when you kick the chair before gambling a 4 cent stamp for the Charles Atlas course, it won't hurt so much!

ON THE ROAD

Your car develops a flat tire on a lonely, deserted road, and to your horror, you find that you have no jack handle.

With Karate, by sheer concentration, you will your index finger into becoming as hard and as rigid as a steel rod.

Which makes it a snap to press the button summoning help!

IN THE CITY

You find yourself in a dark alley, suddenly surrounded by a gang of tough, belligerent, black-jacketed delinquents.

With Karate, you simply channel every ounce of your energy
and strength into the muscles around your mouth and lips —

. — and, as loud as you can, repeat over and over the word —

END

Nowadays, our State and Local Governments employ every conceivable method to raise much needed revenue for highway construction and maintenance—and then use the money for other things. These methods include license fees, gasoline taxes, tolls, and franchises for service stops. One method they've overlooked, which could solve the whole problem and relieve the burden on the already overtaxed automobile owner, would be to contact Madison Avenue, and rent out . . .

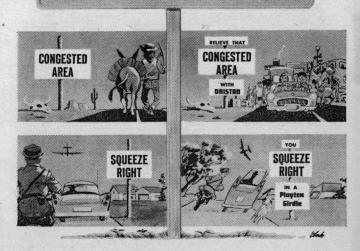

ADVERTISING SPACE ON ROAD SIGNS

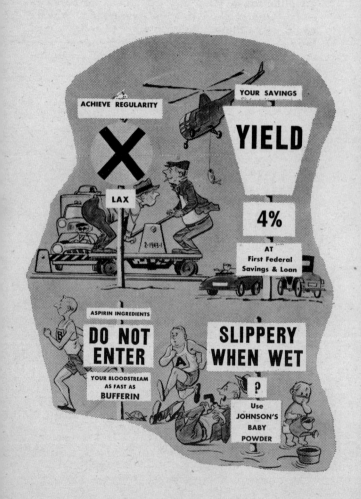

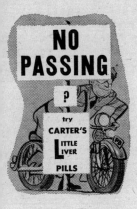

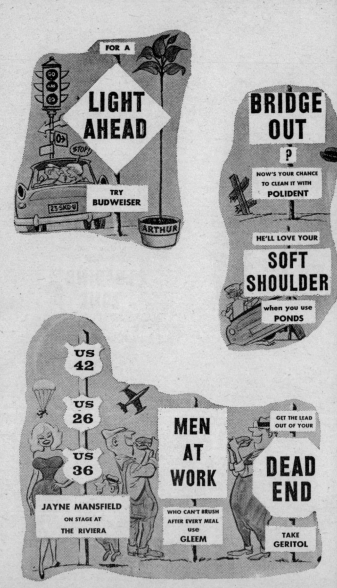

ENJOY

DETOUR

OF SCENIC
BROOKLYN
IN A
**FINSTER
SIGHTSEEING
BUS**

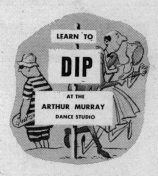

LEARN TO

DIP

AT THE
ARTHUR MURRAY
DANCE STUDIO

**REDUCE
TO
60**

THE NEW
VIC TANNY
WAY

POOF!
THERE GOES
PERSPIRATION!

STOP

ETTE

Most studies of nature are concerned with the descriptions and habits of the various birds, insects and animals, but completely ignore the most important aspect of all—mainly what these creatures are thinking! Not so, however, with—

A
MAD
LOOK AT
NATURE

"I don't have anything against Starlings personally, but when they move into a neighborhood, the property values go down!"

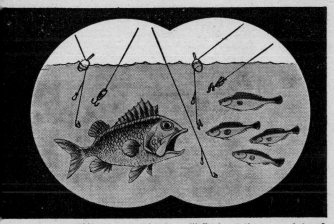

"You new graduates will find out there are lots of things they didn't teach you at the State Hatchery!"

"Hey, Man! Quit buggin' me!"

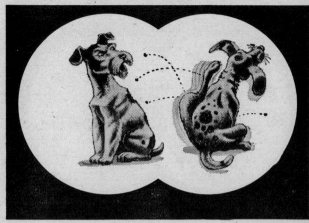

"Son, I think it's time I told you about the birds and the people!"

Somehow, I feel that when you're a millituplet, you sort of lose your personal identity!"

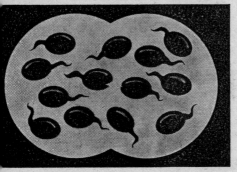

Don't tell me you're that skinny little kid I used to call 'Freckle-Face'. . . !"

"The first few warm days of Spring is the best time to observe their mating habits!"

"... and after the honeymoon, we'll move out to a cute little suburban ranch house ,with pine beams, oak floors, birch cabinets and fir paneling!"

"Baby . . . like I mean, I really dig you!"

"Let's go over to the playground and wait till recess.
It embarrasses the hell out of Miss Jenkins!"

END

We're all familiar with the big fund drives that take place every year, such as <u>The March of Dimes</u>, the <u>Heart Fund</u>, the <u>Muscular Dystrophy Telethon</u>, and like that. We all know these causes are wonderful things that help tremendously in the fight against disease. And we're all <u>for</u> them—hook, line, and wallet! But recently, we learned that there are a lot of <u>other</u> causes which get <u>crowded out</u> by the half-dozen big ones, causes that are just as valid and just as worthwhile! Only they just don't get the same <u>publicity</u>! So, to correct this situation, MAD now throws open its ridiculous pages to promote some of America's...

Little-Known
MEDICAL CRUSADES

Help Put The Squeeze On A Dreaded Disease!

1 OUT OF EVERY 215,630 AMERICANS SUFFERS FROM

BLACKHEADS

DON'T LET IT HAPPEN TO YOU!

How you can help clean out this ugly menace:

(1) Discuss the problem frankly with your family and friends. Remember, "Blackhead" is not a dirty word. It's only a dirty pore!

(2) Get a periodic "Blackhead Check-Up" regularly from your family physician or family barber.

(3) Give generously to "Blackhead Research Projects" in your community. They need your contributions. (Money, that is—not samples!)

(4) Help organize "Soap-And-Water Parties" among the afflicted in your neighborhood.

JOIN
"THE FATHER'S MARCH AGAINST BLACKHEADS"
TODAY!

This Message Prepared as a Public Service by the F.B.I.*

*Fund For Blackhead Immunity

REMEMBER...

I - T Can Strike Anyone!

GIVE GLADLY!
SO THAT OTHERS MAY
LIVE GLADLY!
ANNUAL FUND DRIVE
OF THE
INGROWN TOENAIL APPEAL

If you're not an "Ingrown Toenail Sufferer", you can help stamp out this awful handicap!

(If you are a sufferer, don't try stamping!)

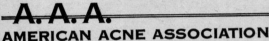

A.A.A.

AMERICAN ACNE ASSOCIATION

August 3rd, 1961

Dear Contributor:--

Another year has gone by, and it's time once more to think of those less fortunate than ourselves...those whose lives have been blighted by the one ailment that causes more people to "lose face" than any other... chronic ACNE.

Can we count on your generous support again this year? We are enclosing a sheet of our beautiful 1961 ACNE STAMPS for pasting on letters, post cards, and old acne scars. In payment, please send whatever you can afford. It will be greatly appreciated.

Remember, you won't be able to look at yourself in the mirror if you let America's acne-sufferers go unaided, if you turn your back on the acne-ridden, or if you happen to develop acne yourself.

Today, more than ever, we Americans must have strength...courage...energy...vision ...and clear complexions if we are to win the "Cold War".

On behalf of millions of adolescents, I remain,

Sufferingly,

Sturdley Thrunch
President, A.A.A.

124

P.N.D. FOUNDATION LAUNCHES FUND AND MEMBERSHIP DRIVE

P.N.D. Foundation President McTouhy

Chicago, Aug. 1— (special to the Times) Dr. Velvl McTouhy, President of the Post Nasal Drip Foundation, announced today the launching of a new campaign designed to make the country Post Nasal Drip conscious.

Dr. McTouhy spoke at the annual P.N.D. Spaghetti Luncheon, held in the elegant Herman J. Klotz Room of the Neuman-Hilton Hotel.

"Post Nasal Drip," said Dr. McTouhy, "is a major threat to the health of our nation. This ailment offers a formidable challenge to medical science because it is so baffling, so dangerous, and mainly —so disgusting!"

Good Evening, Ladies and Gentlemen. This is Jerry Lewis, welcoming you to the sixth annual "Dandruff Telethon"... brought to you by the A.S.D.C.—The American Society for Dandruff Control. We're going to be on the air for the next twenty-four hours—and we'll be shooting for our goal of $250,000...

I know that's a lot of money, folks, but it's for a worthy cause. Just take a look at your watch, and you'll see what I mean. Do you know that every time your watch ticks, somebody in this great land of ours pauses to brush dandruff flakes from his shoulder? Yes, folks, Dandruff Control is a serious and growing problem. Next to the Atomic Bomb, it's the biggest "fallout" problem we've got...

Well, we've got a lot of wonderful talent to entertain you while you're phoning in your pledges, folks. And so, without further ado, I'd like to turn the microphone over to your Master of Ceremonies...a man who richly deserves the place of honor on this Telethon because of all he's done to publicize the problems of Dandruff Control through the years...and here he is...

Yul Brynner!

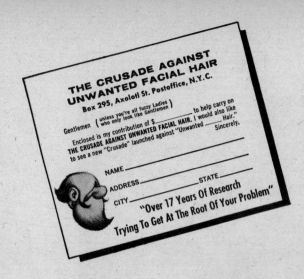

THE CRUSADE AGAINST
UNWANTED FACIAL HAIR

Box 295, Axolotl St. Postoffice, N.Y.C.

Gentlemen (unless you're all fuzzy Ladies)
who only look like Gentlemen

Enclosed is my contribution of $_____ to help carry on
THE CRUSADE AGAINST UNWANTED FACIAL HAIR. I would also like
to see a new "Crusade" launched against "Unwanted _____ Hair."

Sincerely,

NAME_____

ADDRESS_____ STATE_____

CITY_____ "Over 17 Years Of Research
Trying To Get At The Root Of Your Problem"

END

128

Today, America's Space Research Program sorely lacks trained personnel necessary to successfully develop and test advanced **rockets and missiles**. And we're not talking about scientists! We're talking about the men responsible for naming the missiles after the gods and lesser deities of Greek and Roman mythology! Where would our Space Program be without them? To encourage young people into this growing, and extremely important field, our schools should introduce students to the study of mythology at an early age . . . like with—

THE
MAD
mythology
PRIMER

Lesson 1.
PEGASUS

See the horse.
It is a winged horse.
This horse can fly.
Fly; fly, fly.
As if pigeons weren't bad enough!
The horse is named Pegasus.
The jockey is named Bellerophon.
The weather is clear.
The track is fast.
C'mon, Pegasus!
He always finished in the money.
Money, money, money.
Too bad the winged horse isn't alive today.
What a gimmick for a TV western!

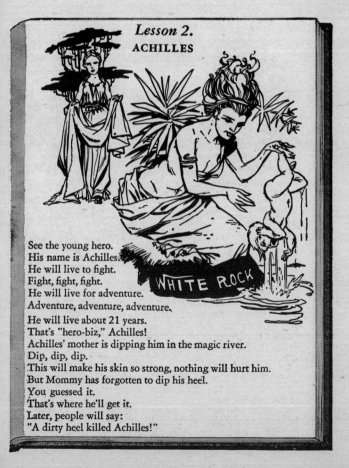

Lesson 2.
ACHILLES

See the young hero.
His name is Achilles.
He will live to fight.
Fight, fight, fight.
He will live for adventure.
Adventure, adventure, adventure.

He will live about 21 years.
That's "hero-biz," Achilles!
Achilles' mother is dipping him in the magic river.
Dip, dip, dip.
This will make his skin so strong, nothing will hurt him.
But Mommy has forgotten to dip his heel.
You guessed it.
That's where he'll get it.
Later, people will say:
"A dirty heel killed Achilles!"

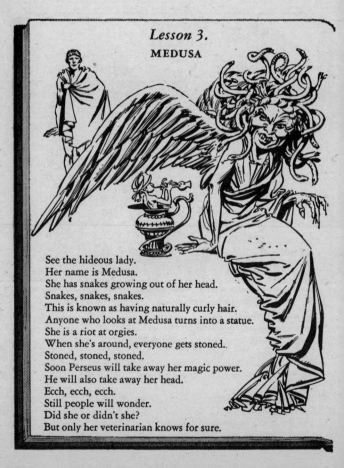

Lesson 3.

MEDUSA

See the hideous lady.
Her name is Medusa.
She has snakes growing out of her head.
Snakes, snakes, snakes.
This is known as having naturally curly hair.
Anyone who looks at Medusa turns into a statue.
She is a riot at orgies.
When she's around, everyone gets stoned.
Stoned, stoned, stoned.
Soon Perseus will take away her magic power.
He will also take away her head.
Ecch, ecch, ecch.
Still people will wonder.
Did she or didn't she?
But only her veterinarian knows for sure.

Lesson 4.
KING MIDAS

See the King.
His name is King Midas.
King Midas is very greedy.
Greedy, greedy, greedy.
Today, he would be playing the Stock Market.
Midas has magic power.
Magic, magic, magic.
Everything he touches turns to gold.
Gold, gold, gold.
Some day, a mosquito will bite King Midas on his stomach.
Scratch, scratch, scratch.
Whoops! A 22-carat belly-button.

133

Lesson 5.
THE CENTAUR

See the strange creature.
He is half man, half horse.
He is called a Centaur.
The Centaur is very silly.
Silly, silly, silly.
He is always chasing girls.
And he drinks too much.
And he sings and dances all day.
And he can't hold a steady job.
Boy, how silly can you get!
The Centaur is extinct today.
But his descendents are still around.
They live in Hollywood.

Lesson 6.
ECHO AND NARCISSUS

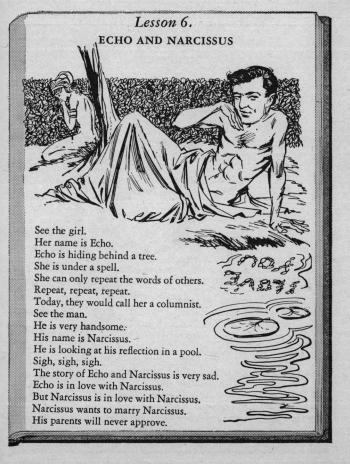

See the girl.
Her name is Echo.
Echo is hiding behind a tree.
She is under a spell.
She can only repeat the words of others.
Repeat, repeat, repeat.
Today, they would call her a columnist.
See the man.
He is very handsome.
His name is Narcissus.
He is looking at his reflection in a pool.
Sigh, sigh, sigh.
The story of Echo and Narcissus is very sad.
Echo is in love with Narcissus.
But Narcissus is in love with Narcissus.
Narcissus wants to marry Narcissus.
His parents will never approve.

Lesson 7.

HERCULES

See the man.
His name is Hercules.
Hercules has huge muscles.
This makes him look very strong.
Strong, strong, strong.
Hercules wears the skin of a dead lion.
This makes him smell very strong.
Smell, smell, smell.
Hercules has to perform twelve labors.
One of them is to clean out the Augean Stables.
This doesn't help the situation much.
Someday, they will make movies about Hercules.
Movies, movies, movies.
These movies will carry on the Hercules tradition.
They will also smell.

136

Lesson 8.

THE TROJAN HORSE

See the big horse.
The horse is made of wood.
Clever Greek soldiers are hiding inside the horse.
Hide, hide, hide.
Today, the Trojans will roll the horse into the city.
Tonight, there will be a surprise party in the city.
Tomorrow, there will be a fire sale in the city.
Later, some Trojans will say:
    "Beware of Greeks bearing gifts."
While some others will say,
    "Beware of gifts bearing Greeks!"
This incident will make Troy famous.
Troy will be known as the first "one-horse town."

Lesson 9.

PLUTO

See the evil man.
His name is Pluto.
He is King of the Dead.
Boo, hiss, boo.
Pluto is the undisputed Ruler of the Underworld.
Sort of a mythological Frank Nitti.
But Pluto is very unhappy.
Unhappy, unhappy, unhappy.
He doesn't like being King of the Dead.
Because he can't tell his subjects where to go.
They're already there.

Lesson 10.
ULYSSES

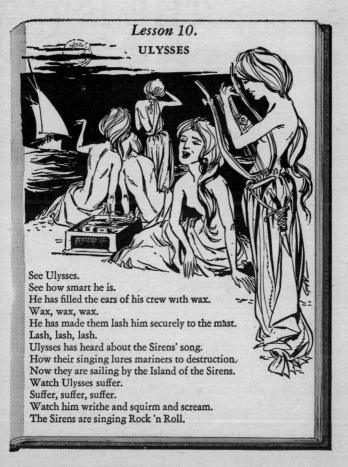

See Ulysses.
See how smart he is.
He has filled the ears of his crew with wax.
Wax, wax, wax.
He has made them lash him securely to the mast.
Lash, lash, lash.
Ulysses has heard about the Sirens' song.
How their singing lures mariners to destruction.
Now they are sailing by the Island of the Sirens.
Watch Ulysses suffer.
Suffer, suffer, suffer.
Watch him writhe and squirm and scream.
The Sirens are singing Rock 'n Roll.

E N D

We noticed that Don Martin, MAD's maddest artist, has been "jumpy" lately . . . so we asked him about it. He told us that it all began with:

THE P^OG^O

-STICK

INCIDENT

American Telephone and Telegraph (AT&T) is a mammoth corporation dedicated to the improvement of communications. In this task, they have succeeded admirably. Take, for example, their fantastic scientific breakthrough of several years ago, when a stunned world received news of the development of the first color telephone. Think of the millions of dollars in research that went into this marvelous electronic advance. And more recently, we witnessed the introduction of another scientific wonder—the "Princess" phone. Not only is it beautiful to behold, but it contains the marvel of a built-in light. Just imagine the advantage of dimming the houselights, and dial to the warm and enchanting glow of the remarkable "Princess." Can Russia and her 4-ton "Sputniks" ever hope to match this remarkable scientific achievement? But the best is yet to come as MAD now reveals—

FUTURE TELEPHONE TRIUMPHS

THE "BLACK BEAUTY" PHONE

Classic Design and Function

This instrument does not do a thing, except carry phone messages quickly and efficiently. It is simple to operate, comfortable to hold, occupies little space, and looks like exactly what it is supposed to be. It is cheap to make, and inexpensive to rent. It is also impossible to get!

THE "SPECIAL

THE
"IMPERSONATOR"
PHONE
Electronic Voice Changer

This marvelous instrument has countless advantages. The speaker, simply by manipulating dials, can make his voice sound any way he pleases. Here are just a few of the ways this device can be used. Only $37.75 extra monthly charge.

SELECTING THE PROPER VOICE CAN BE INVALUABLE IN

ROMANCE

DEVICES" LINE

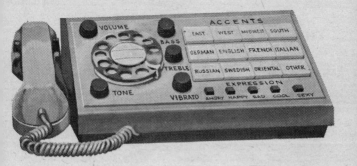

BUSINESS

GETTING OUT OF JAMS

THE "NERVESAVER" PHONE

Automatic Dial Tone Indicator

The busy person who is always annoyed at having to wait for the dial tone will welcome this new telephone. Merely press the button, and dial tone contact is automatically made without lifting receiver. When this happens, a light flashes, and dialing can begin. Only $8.00 extra per mo. (There is a humorous twist to the story of this amazing new invention. Actually, two huge phone company labs were working on this problem. Both came up with solutions: the one shown here, and another which accomplished the same thing on existing phones. Naturally, the latter idea was quickly abandoned when the company suddenly realized that there could be no extra monthly carrying charge for that!)

THE "SYMPHONETTE" PHONE

Musical Busy Signaller

No more being bored and frustrated with irritating busy-signals. This instrument brings a continuous flow of soft, soothing music when phone at other end of line is in use. Many people, it is hoped, will deliberately dial numbers they know are busy, just to hear this lovely music treat. Only $1.00 per busy signal dialed, plus 25¢ per minute.

THE "SMELLSWEET" PHONE

Offensive Odor Controller

This new development is a practical boon to people with extra-sensitive noses who can't stand the offensive odors deposited on mouthpieces by prior users of phones. Button releases fragrant mist from hidden vial in headpiece when pressed. Phone only $10.00 extra monthly charge. Vials of fragrant mist only $3.00 each — last for days, depending on number of offensive-breathed people who use the phone.

THE "AUDIO-FAKER" PHONE

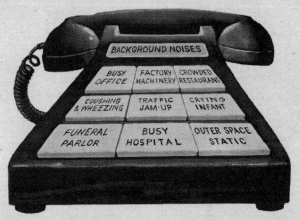

Background Sound Producer

This remarkable phone contains a tiny tape recorder which, at the touch of a button, introduces authentic background sounds while conversation is going on. The merits of this device are painfully obvious to any husband who has ever called his wife to say he's working late at the office — and in the background, she hears drunks raving and girls giggling. Now, all he need do is press the "Busy Office" background noises button, and his wife hears the clatter of typewriters and adding machines. Or take the guy who wants to take the day off to play golf. All he need do is press the "Coughing and Wheezing" button when calling in to talk to the boss. Only $15.00 per month extra charge.

NOW IN THE FINAL ST

THE "ROYAL" LINE

The success of the revolutionary "color" phone encouraged
continued work along those lines. Research scientists by

THE "KING" PHONE

THE "QUEEN" PHONE

For Dad—the regal splendor
of this attractive phone is
designed to give the head-
man a feeling of importance.

For Mom—the quiet dignity
of this magnificent phone
indicates who is actually
the power behind the throne.

AGES OF DEVELOPMENT

the thousands were hired at great expense (to lure them away from military defense projects), with these results:

THE "COURTESAN" PHONE	THE "DRAGON" PHONE

For that personal secretary, or that pretty maid, or any other female the king might wish to honor with a reward.

For that Mother-In-Law, her very own receiver, so she'll spend hours on it, thus keeping her off everybody's neck.

SOME ASTOUNDING TELE

THE "DECORATOR" LINE

The success of the amazing "Princess" naturally inspired the company to create a whole line of "Royal" receivers.

Proud

Fun

"THE HIGHLANDER"

For telephone subscribers of Scotch ancestry, tartan patterns of all known clans will be available (for only $3.00 extra monthly charge).

"THE BLECCHHH"

For subscribers with kids, plastic will simulate jam, peanut butter, etc. Doesn't show mess like other phones. ($4.00 extra monthly charge)

PHONE ADVANCEMENTS

Soon, every home can be a palace, with special phones for each member (at the low extra charge of $7 monthly each).

Stimulating

"THE VAVAVAVOOM"

For the bachelor subscriber to dress up his penthouse. Adds an inspirational mood to little black book work. ($5.00 extra monthly charge).

Functional

"THE MINDSAVER"

Most-used numbers imbedded in plastic phone for quick reference. Numbers changed for slight $25.00 service charge. ($6.00 per month).

For our first peek into the "butt-end-down mind" of Don Martin, here is his version of the period in his life when he was known as

THE INVE

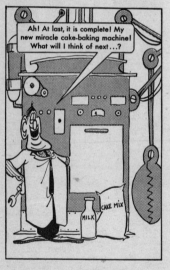

Ah! At last, it is complete! My new miracle cake-baking machine! What will I think of next...?

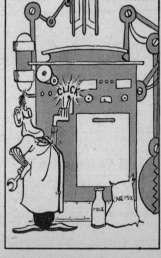

CLICK

NTOR

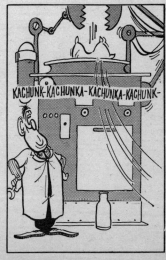

KACHUNKA-KACHUNKA-KACHUNK-KACHUNK-

KACHUNK- KACHUNKA-KACHUNK-KACHUNK-

E N D

CONDENSED MILKING DEPT.

And now, MAD presents its version of the famous monthly magazine that once took pride in the fact that it did not accept advertising, only now it's filled with advertising . . . that once listed all its articles on the front cover, only now it lists them on its back cover . . . and once was a pretty corny magazine, only now it's even cornier . . .

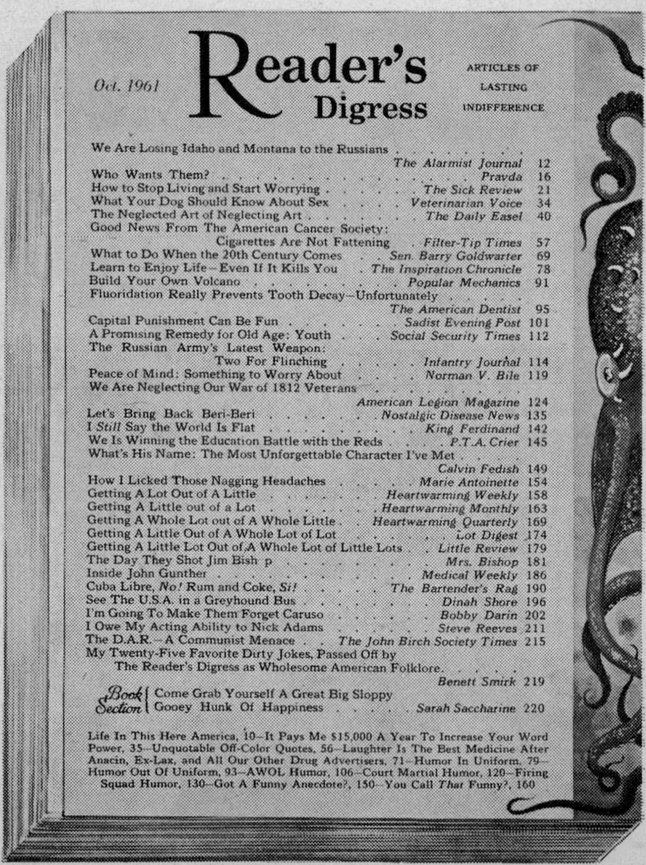

Oct. 1961

Reader's Digress

ARTICLES OF LASTING INDIFFERENCE

We Are Losing Idaho and Montana to the Russians . . . . *The Alarmist Journal* 12
Who Wants Them? . . . . *Pravda* 16
How to Stop Living and Start Worrying . . . . . . *The Sick Review* 21
What Your Dog Should Know About Sex . . . . *Veterinarian Voice* 34
The Neglected Art of Neglecting Art . . . . *The Daily Easel* 40
Good News From The American Cancer Society: Cigarettes Are Not Fattening . *Filter-Tip Times* 57
What to Do When the 20th Century Comes . . *Sen. Barry Goldwarter* 69
Learn to Enjoy Life—Even If It Kills You . *The Inspiration Chronicle* 78
Build Your Own Volcano . . . . *Popular Mechanics* 91
Fluoridation Really Prevents Tooth Decay—Unfortunately . . . . . *The American Dentist* 95
Capital Punishment Can Be Fun . . . . *Sadist Evening Post* 101
A Promising Remedy for Old Age: Youth . . . *Social Security Times* 112
The Russian Army's Latest Weapon: Two For Flinching . . . . . *Infantry Journal* 114
Peace of Mind: Something to Worry About . . . . *Norman V. Bile* 119
We Are Neglecting Our War of 1812 Veterans . . . . *American Legion Magazine* 124
Let's Bring Back Beri-Beri . . . . *Nostalgic Disease News* 135
I *Still* Say the World Is Flat . . . . *King Ferdinand* 142
We Is Winning the Education Battle with the Reds . . . . *P.T.A. Crier* 145
What's His Name: The Most Unforgettable Character I've Met . . . . *Calvin Fedish* 149
How I Licked Those Nagging Headaches . . . . . *Marie Antoinette* 154
Getting A Lot Out of A Little . . . . *Heartwarming Weekly* 158
Getting A Little out of a Lot . . . . . . *Heartwarming Monthly* 163
Getting A Whole Lot out of A Whole Little . . *Heartwarming Quarterly* 169
Getting A Little Out of A Whole Lot of Lot . . . . . . *Lot Digest* 174
Getting A Little Lot Out of A Whole Lot of Little Lots . . *Little Review* 179
The Day They Shot Jim Bish p . . . . *Mrs. Bishop* 181
Inside John Gunther . . . . *Medical Weekly* 186
Cuba Libre, *No!* Rum and Coke, *Si!* . . . . . *The Bartender's Rag* 190
See The U.S.A. in a Greyhound Bus . . . . *Dinah Shore* 196
I'm Going To Make Them Forget Caruso . . . . . . *Bobby Darin* 202
I Owe My Acting Ability to Nick Adams . . . . . . *Steve Reeves* 211
The D.A.R.—A Communist Menace . . *The John Birch Society Times* 215
My Twenty-Five Favorite Dirty Jokes, Passed Off by The Reader's Digress as Wholesome American Folklore. . . . . . *Benett Smirk* 219

Book Section Come Grab Yourself A Great Big Sloppy Gooey Hunk Of Happiness . . . . . *Sarah Saccharine* 220

Life In This Here America, 10—It Pays Me $15,000 A Year To Increase Your Word Power, 35—Unquotable Off-Color Quotes, 56—Laughter Is The Best Medicine After Anacin, Ex-Lax, and All Our Other Drug Advertisers, 71—Humor In Uniform, 79—Humor Out Of Uniform, 93—AWOL Humor, 106—Court Martial Humor, 120—Firing Squad Humor, 130—Got A Funny Anecdote?, 150—You Call *That* Funny?, 160

The Echoes of Mankind

BY SELWIN R. ZABINDIN
President, Consolidated Money, Inc.

ONE DAY, A FAMOUS AUTHOR and lecturer was seated next to a slight, gray-haired old lady aboard a jet airliner. Leaning toward the woman, the author smiled and whispered, "The echoes of mankind are irrepressible."

Whereupon the sweet old lady's kindly eyes twinkled, and she replied, "Go fish a herring!"

What, you may ask, does a whimsical anecdote have to do with introducing an inside-front-cover endorsement for The Reader's Digress? I don't know! They all seem to start that way, so why should mine be any different?

Why am I an avid reader of the Digress?

Because the editors have an uncanny method of going through lengthy works, and reprinting those parts which they consider important—while ignoring those parts which they consider unimportant. This is inspired editing.

It is also crass censorship.

But being a busy, high-powered executive, I don't have the time to read things through, so I let the Digress tell me what *they* think I should read. This is the mark of a realistic, time-saving, knowledge-hungry citizen.

It is also the mark of a true ignoramus.

I can't tell you how delighted I am with this great publication. And how even more delighted I am to grab this page ahead of hundreds of other distinguished business executives, who are also anxious to plug their corporations here and save themselves thousands of dollars in advertising.

This cover endorsement, like everything else I do in and out of the business world, comes directly from my heart. And I couldn't feel more strongly and more sincere about it...even if I had written it myself.

Reader's Digress

Appears Reg.
U.S. Nws. Stds.
Marka Illiteracy

VOL. 78, NO. 472, October, 1961   Published each month simultaneously in the United States by The Reader's Digress Association, Inc., Pleasantlife, N. Y., and in Canada by its Canadian subsidiary, and in England by its English subsidiary, and in France by its French subsidiary, and in every other country in the world where we can pass off this tripe as interesting reading matter, and get several billion gullible people to pay 35 cents a copy, and $4.00 a year for it.

Humor in Service

AN ABSOLUTELY HILARIOUS thing happened to me during World War II when I was stationed in the Philippines. One day, just before an important battle, I complained to my First Sergeant that I was homesick. He told me what to do about it, and I thanked him profusely. I packed my things, caught a plane back to the States, and went directly to Hollywood, California.

When I was picked up by the M.P.'s a month later, and brought back to my First Sergeant, he said, "What in #$%& happened to you?"

"Well, last month I *told* you I was homesick," I reminded him.

"Sure," he said, "and I told you to tell it to the Chaplain! You know— the *Army* Chaplain! It's a G.I. expression meaning 'Ain't that *too bad!*'"

"Oh, you meant the ARMY Chaplain?" I said, starting to giggle. "I thought you meant, tell it to CHARLIE Chaplin!"

Everyone laughed so hard at this that it took the firing squad a good half hour to compose themselves and aim their rifles at me properly.

— PVT. SAUL FLEEBLE (*Arlington Cemetery*)

IN JUNE, 1944, I was in a Basic Training Camp in Georgia, when a riotously funny incident took place. My first Sergeant, a huge fellow well over six feet tall and weighing 250 pounds, walked into our barracks, sobbing.

"I just got a 'Dear John' letter fróm my wife," he said, choking back the tears. "She sold my house, my car, all my belongings, took our five kids, and ran off with a black market operator to New Zealand."

Suddenly, I began to chuckle. Then my chuckle turned to laughter, and my laughter turned to uncontrolled roars of hysteria. I doubled up and rolled back and forth on the floor, nearly drowning in my tears of mirth.

He looked at me strangely, and said, "What's so funny about me getting a 'Dear John' letter from my wife?"

"That...that...that's one on her!" I said, gasping for breath. "YOUR name is *Murray!*"

When he walked out of the barracks a few moments later, I was still laughing. But I stopped momentarily to pick up 14 of my teeth.

— GEORGE "GUMMY" VOLDUZZI (*Gary, Ind.*)

IN JANUARY, 1945, our Infantry Division was ordered to take an important mountain peak in Italy. We attacked at dawn, advanced half-way up the slope, and then were forced to retreat because the shelling was so fierce. Casualties on both sides were quite heavy. Three hours later, we attacked again, and once more the shelling was fierce. But we managed to battle our way to the top and gain control of the mountain. Losses on both sides were very heavy.

On re-reading the preceding anecdote, I've decided that perhaps it isn't as humorous as others I've read in The Reader's Digress, but I'm sending it to the "Humor In Service" editor anyway.

After all, there are lots of ex-G.I.s who think war isn't so funny!

— CHARLIE FRANK (*Augusta, Ga.*)

I Licked Chapped Lips

A middle-aged man's courageous battle over one of mankind's most baffling medical enigmas

Condensed from
The American Medical Journal
BY EDWARD MOSH
as told to Dr. Morris Fishbein
who wouldn't listen

AS I BUTTONED my shirt in the doctor's office, an uncomfortable dryness clutched at my throat.

"Give it to me straight, Doc," I said.

"Mr. Mosh," he began quietly, "my tests prove conclusively that you are suffering from a severe case of chapped lips—upper right and lower left labial regions."

I leaned forward, gripping his desk so tight my knuckles turned white. "How...how long until it's all over?" I stammered.

He shrugged. "A week perhaps. A month. It could even go on all winter. And then, it may return in a year. We never know about these things. Try not to worry."

Try not to worry, indeed! In a stupor, I staggered home. As soon as my wife saw me, she *knew*. "Ed," she said stoutly, fighting back the tears, "you're going to *fight* this thing, and I'm going to *help* you."

"*You?*" I laughed bitterly. "What can *you* do? What can *anyone* do?

Nobody licks chapped lips! It has to run its course! A week, a month, the whole winter! And then, there's always next year..."

"We can lick it with a little *help*," my wife said softly, gazing upward.

"You mean...?" I said, following her upward gaze.

"Yes," she said, continuing to look upward.

"You mean...?" I repeated, continuing to look upward too.

During the next few months, thanks to faith, hope, courage, and trust in our upstairs neighbor, Sadie Mueller, who lent me her "ChapStick," I LICKED CHAPPED LIPS!

And as dreadful as my experience was, if this article can give other unfortunate human beings the inspiration to conquer *their* afflictions, it was worth it.

It was also worth $2500.

NEXT MONTH: HOW I LICKED ATHLETE'S FEET

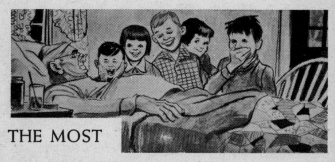

THE MOST

MEMORABLE CHARACTER I'VE MET

YET EVER TILL NOW By Samuel Quintz

ONE OF US in Sackinaw, Kentucky, will ever forget my eccentric old grandfather. What a memorable character that unpredictable, lovable old fellow was!

He was such an irresistible cut-up that we gave him a special nickname. We used to call him "Grandpa." Somehow, the name just fit the peculiar old codger. My grandmother, however, had her own pet name for him, which was no less descriptive. She used to call him "Harold," which always gave us a good laugh.

I'll never forget the first time Grandpa met my wife-to-be, Alice. "Well, how do you like her, Grandpa?" I asked him, bracing myself for his usual unpredictable answer.

"She seems rather nice, Sam," he said not batting an eye. I suppose I'd have been shocked had I not been so used to his unexpected gibes.

Any time he was hungry, Grandpa would walk into the kitchen and cause the wildest commotion with acid comments like "May I eat now, please?" And whenever he was ready to put on a pair of shoes, you could rest assured the eccentric old duck would first put on something insane, like a pair of socks.

The day before Grandpa's 84th birthday, Old Doc Barnes, who was visiting us, stopped by Grandpa's room to say hello. Imagine our surprise when he told us Grandpa had been dead for two years.

"No wonder he never touched the soup last Thanksgiving," said Grandma.

We buried Grandpa. He would have wanted it that way, character that he was.

Somehow, things just aren't the same these days in Grandma's house in Sackinaw.

But I forget why.

How I Ease My Everyday Tensions

*All of us need to find
refuge from the stresses, strains,
demands, and jarring uncertainties of
20th Century living. One housewife
offers an inspirational
answer*

Condensed from

Lamplighter Magazine

(Where it will appear next month, because we had it
planted there in the first place)

FRANCIS KVOORTZ

LIKE MOST PEOPLE in this unpredict-able Atomic Age, I, too, was filled with the usual nagging strains and tensions of life. They hounded and tortured me constantly through the day as I went about the task of caring for my home and family and goldfish and parakeet.

But one day, after long years of torment, I finally discovered how to cope with these tensions. And finding this heart-warming, wonderful remedy has meant a world of difference to me as a wife, a mother, a part-time veterinarian, and a human being.

Twice a day, during the busiest part of my house-work schedule, I stop all activity, remove my apron, and sit down on a couch. The first thing I do is meditate. I think about my past life, my present life, and what the future may hold in store for me. I think about my home, my husband, the children, and the life we have together. I think about the warm, richly-optimistic articles I've read in The Reader's Digress, which have reminded me about these blessings.

And then, suddenly, a warm feeling wells up inside me. It makes me forget everything else that has happened during the day. It makes me feel alive, conscious of my surroundings, determined in my direction. Soon, I feel as if a tremendous weight has been lifted from me. Refreshed, I am ready to come to grips with the world once more.

How do I ease my everyday tensions? I throw up.

WHILE MOTORING through New Mexico last summer, my wife and I saw a teepee standing by the side of the road. Seated in front of the teepee was an authentic-looking Indian, gaudily painted and wearing a colorful tribal headdress.

We stopped the car and approached him. "Ask him in sign language if he sells souvenirs," my wife whispered.

Pointing my finger at him, I said, "You…" Then I held up a string of beads and dangled them before his eyes. Finally I took out some money and waved it in front of his face.

The Indian smiled faintly, looking first at me and then at my wife.

"Ugh!" he grunted.

As old Reader's Digress fans, we were stunned and shocked. Not only didn't this Indian speak perfect English, but we found out later that he didn't even come from Brooklyn.

— MARVIN ZULTE (*Worcester, Mass.*)

I WAS VISITING New York City for the first time, and I decided to take my first subway ride. So I boarded a train at Times Square one weekday at 5:00 P.M. Needless to say, the train was jammed with people, all pushing and shoving and using dreadful language. However, off in a corner, I happened to notice a kindly-looking elderly man standing amid the crush with a warm smile on his face.

Squeezing through the mob of screaming, perspiring, cursing passengers, I managed to get near enough to the smiling old gentleman to say, "Pardon me, sir. I can't help noticing how good-naturedly you seem to be taking this dreadful subway ride. How is it that you can view the whole situation with a sly sense of humor, while all those around you are working themselves up into a frenzy of hate?"

The old man looked at me with twinkling eyes, then tapped his head gently with a forefinger, and said softly, "I'm sick!"

— MEL HANRY (*Cokeville, Wyo.*)

A FEW WEEKS AGO, at the Dayton, Ohio, Dog Pound, we received this letter, printed in a childish hand:

Dere Dog Ketchers,

My name is Joey Harris. I am seven yeers old. Every day, I see you ketch doggs and gass them dead.

I am lonesume, and I don't have no one to play with, and I don't have no dogg.

Instead of gassing one of the doggs, could you please give him to me. I will love him and take care of him and play with him, even if he is a skinny little mutt.

Your frennd,
Joey

There wasn't a dry eye in the whole Dog Pound as we composed the following answer to little Joey:

"No!"

— HERMAN BRUGGER (*Dayton, Ohio*)

END

It Pays to Decrease Your
WORD POWER

By Wilfred Fink

IT'S A FACT that the most successful businessmen today are also the most illiterate. If you want to be successful, it's important to decrease your vocabulary. Check the word or phrase below that is *farthest in meaning* from the key word. Do this every issue—eventually it will become a *habit*—and you'll end up *stupid, but rich.*

Toward
More Picturesque Talking, Like

CAAAAAAAASH Clothes! (Irving, a traveling old clothes buyer, in a Street) . . . Hey, bananooooooos! Two pouns ferra quaarter! (Vito, a fruit vendor, in the Same Street) . . . Maaa! Trow me down money forda moom pitchers! (Seymour, in a backyard) . . . Come up first and drink your milk or I'll smash your head against a wall till you bleed! (Mother, in a Backyard Window) . . . Aaahhh, shaddup, the whole two of yuh! (Gus Popovski, on a Fire Escape) . . .

Heart-Warming Filler

ONE DAY, A FRECKLE-FACED LITTLE BOY, eating a wholesome piece of apple pie made by Mom, was walking with a friendly, but homeless dog named Spot. Suddenly, the boy and the dog caught sight of a little, kindly, gray-haired old lady with shining eyes . . . So far, this much alone is enough to make The Reader's Digress, so I believe I'll save my punch line for another anecdote.

—Arnold Lovelace, quoted by *Leonard Lyons*

Unquotable Quotes

A FRIEND in need is best considered an enemy.

—Ben Folgarth, quoted in *The Selfish Eve. Post*

LOVE thy neighbor as you do thy wife.

—George Jessel, in *Boy's Life*

IT'S BETTER to have loved and lost; it's also cheaper.

—Dick Foran, in *The Sears Roebuck Catalogue*

IN SPRING, an old man's stomach turns.

—Chester A. Arthur, in *Army Laffs*

GONE WITH THE WIND

BY MARGARET MITCHELL

The Reader's Digress one-page condensation of a 1,037 page classic, which is so detailed and complete, thanks to our superb Condensed Books Editing Staff, that reading the original would be an absolute waste of time

"IT LOOKS LIKE WAR, Miss Scarlett," said the Tarleton twins.

"Fiddle-dee-dee," said Scarlett O'Hara.

Boom!

"Thank God that bloody war is .over," said Rhett Butler. "Will you marry me, Scarlett?"

"No."

"Well, if it's going to come to this constant bickering, let's forget it."

"Ashley," said Scarlett, "it's *you* I love!"

"But I'm married to Melanie," he answered. "Besides, we've got a war to win first."

"Don't be silly," said Scarlett.

"The war ended right after 'Fiddle-dee-dee' and 'Boom'!"

"So you married Frank Kennedy, eh, Scarlett?" Rhett sneered.

"Yes, but he died," Scarlett pouted.

"Time flies," mused Rhett.

"I need you, Rhett."

"I'm sorry, Scarlett. Our marriage isn't working out. Besides, I've got a war to fight."

"Don't be silly. The Civil War ended just after 'Fiddle-dee-dee' and 'Boom'!"

"What kind Civil War?" barked Rhett. "We've been moving so fast, it's time for World War I already!"

There's been a lot of talk lately about how Americans are getting soft. Escalators, power steering, and push-button appliances are making life too easy for us. A recent network television documentary called "The Flabby American," called for a national physical fitness program to get people interested in exercising. Which is all very well, except that we at MAD know how it is with exercising. After all, how many push-ups can you do before the novelty wears off? What we need is to change America's living habits, and make people exercise unconsciously—by adopting . . .

MAD'S
PHYSICAL
FITNESS
PROGRAM

High Straps on Busses and Trains

Parking Meters on Tall Poles

"Push" Signs on "Pull" Doors
(and vice versa)

Teeny Tiny Numbers on Scales

Front Doors Without Steps

Heavy Telephone Receivers

High Safety Islands

Strong Springs on Mail Box Lids

CLANGK

THWUNK

Raised Ticket Office Windows

Bigger and Better Issues of MAD

END

THEY ALSO SURF
WHO ONLY SAND AND WADE DEPT.

Every summer, millions of Americans escape the heat by crowding onto the nation's beaches. Well, the heat's on again! Because, be it lake shore or sea shore, you can be darn shore there'll be idiotic behavior like the following episodes, comprising —

A
MAD
LOOK

AT THE BEACH

A beach is the place
Where all shapes and sizes
Lack girdles and padding
To make their disguises!

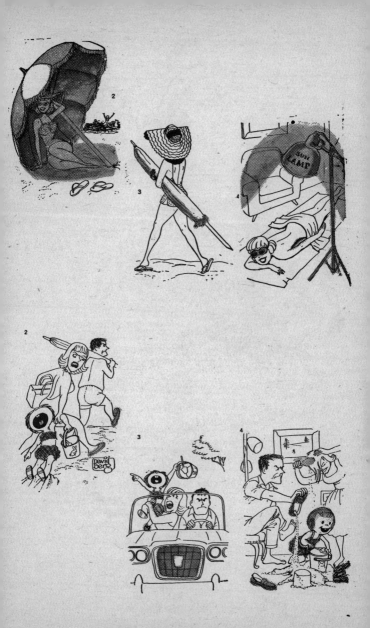

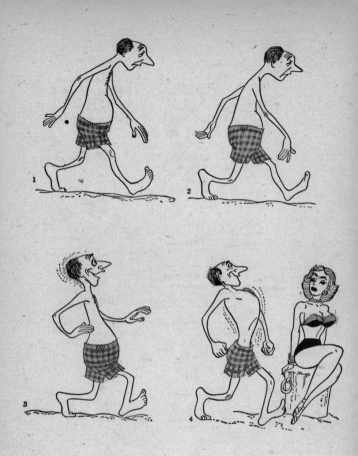

End